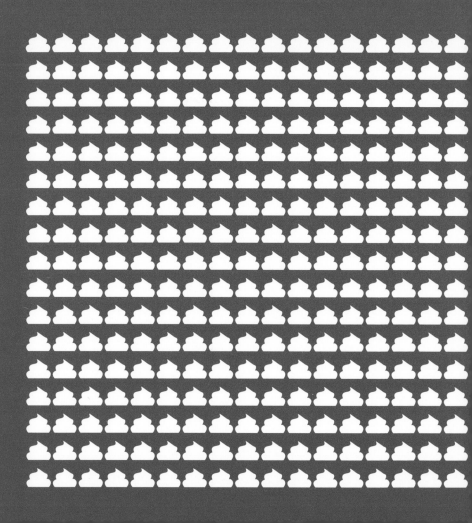

For your bathroom in Twickenham!

:)

Lx

52 POODOKUS TO DO WHILE YOU POO

Xmas '15

SUMMERSDALE PUBLISHERS LTD
46 WEST STREET
CHICHESTER
WEST SUSSEX
PO19 1RP
UK

WWW.SUMMERSDALE.COM
PRINTED AND BOUND IN CHINA
ISBN: 978-1-84953-767-4

SUBSTANTIAL DISCOUNTS ON BULK QUANTITIES OF SUMMERSDALE BOOKS
ARE AVAILABLE TO CORPORATIONS, PROFESSIONAL ASSOCIATIONS AND OTHER
ORGANISATIONS. FOR DETAILS CONTACT NICKY DOUGLAS BY TELEPHONE:
+44 (0) 1243 756902, FAX: +44 (0) 1243 786300 OR EMAIL: NICKY@SUMMERSDALE.COM

POODOKU
DIFFICULTY LEVEL 💩💩💩

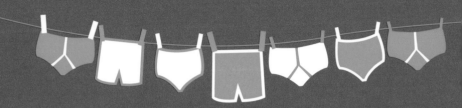

POODOKU
DIFFICULTY LEVEL 💩💩💩

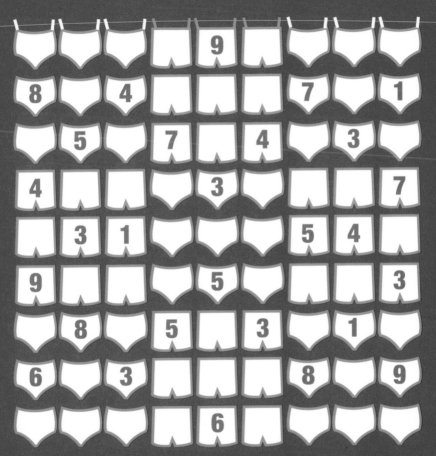

POODOKU
DIFFICULTY LEVEL

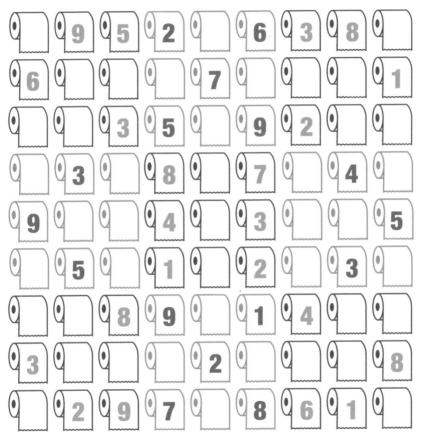

POODOKU
DIFFICULTY LEVEL

52 POODOKUS TO DO...

5				2				7
			9		5			
9			7		1			2
	2			6			3	
	6		5		4		2	
	7			9			4	
6			8		7			9
			2		9			
2				3				8

POODOKU

DIFFICULTY LEVEL 💩 💩 💩

52 POODOKUS TO DO...

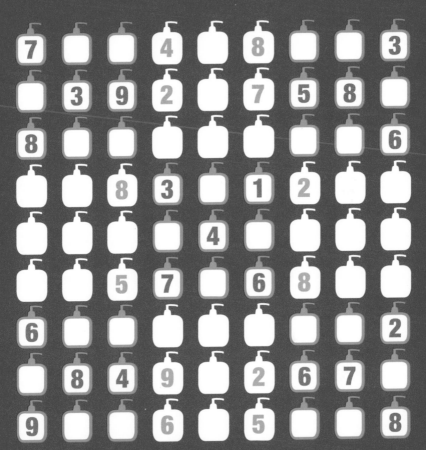

POODOKU
DIFFICULTY LEVEL 💩 △ △

	PEE	WAZ	PISS		
PISS			WEE	WAZ	PEE
				PISS	
	PISS		WAZ		TINKLE
URINATE	WAZ			WEE	PISS
TINKLE		PISS		PEE	

POODOKU
DIFFICULTY LEVEL 💩💩💩

POODOKU
DIFFICULTY LEVEL

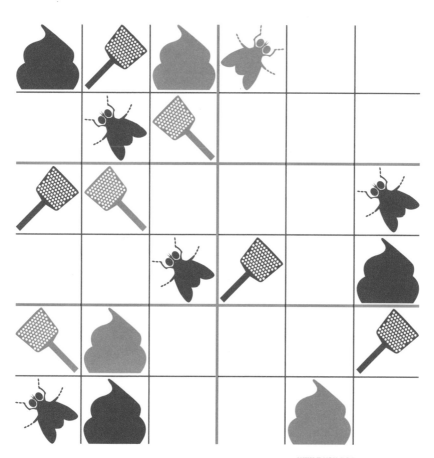

POODOKU
DIFFICULTY LEVEL

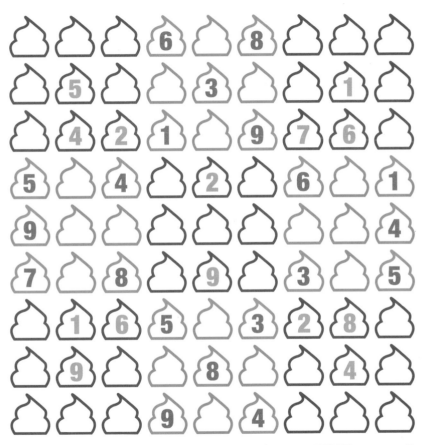

POODOKU
DIFFICULTY LEVEL 💩🔺🔺

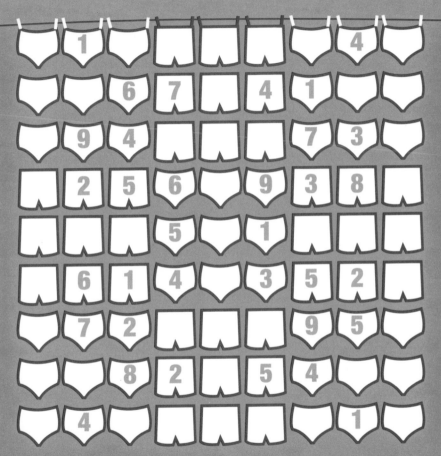

POODOKU
DIFFICULTY LEVEL 💩💩💩

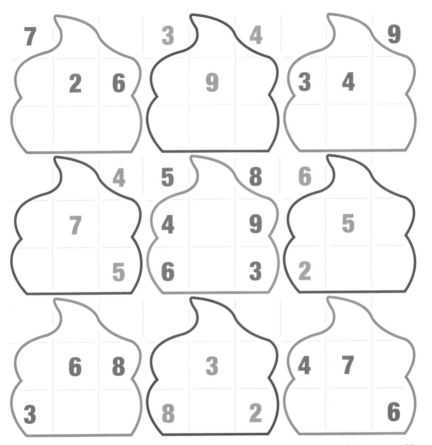

EACH ICON SHOULD APPEAR ONCE IN EVERY ROW, COLUMN AND 3X2 BOX

POODOKU
DIFFICULTY LEVEL

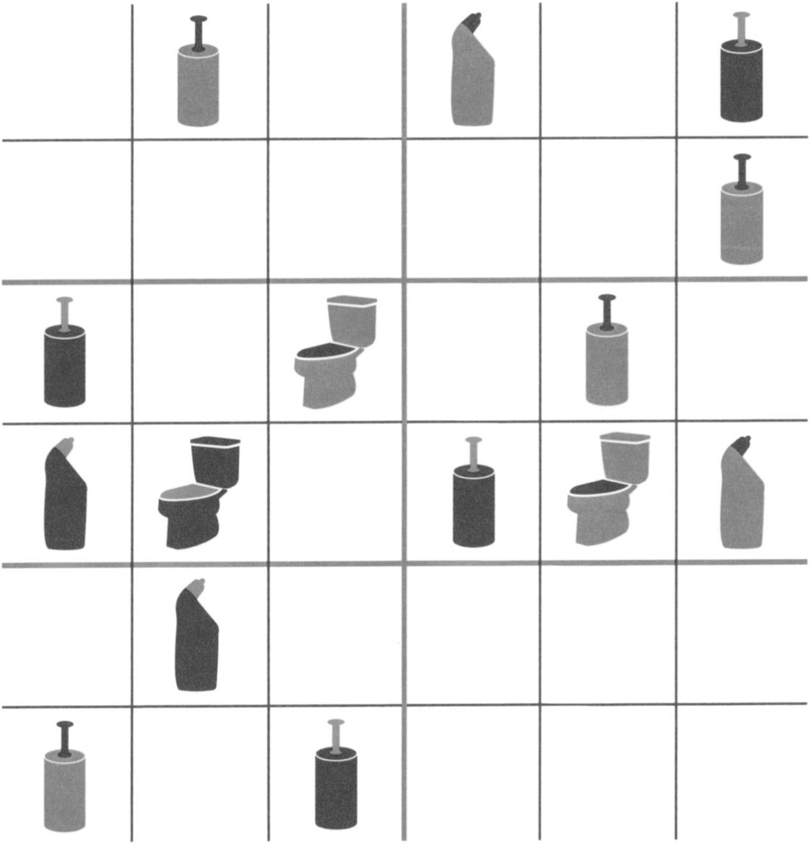

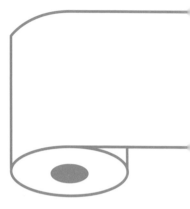

POODOKU
DIFFICULTY LEVEL ▲ △ △

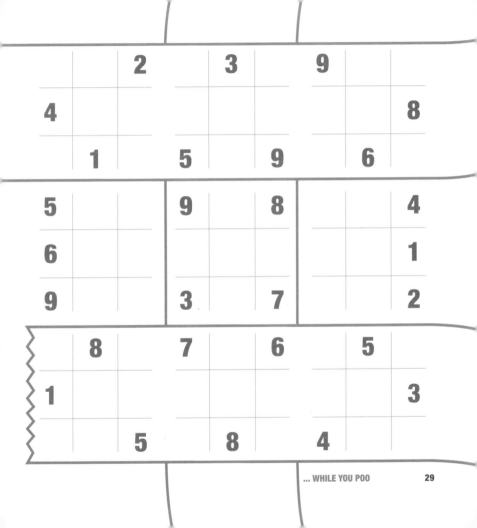

POODOKU
DIFFICULTY LEVEL

	Y	!		V		A	O	
L	V						Y	!
T	A		A		L		!	Y
			R		T			
Y	O		!		V		A	T
V	!						R	O
	L	A		!		Y	T	

POODOKU
DIFFICULTY LEVEL 💩 🔺 🔺

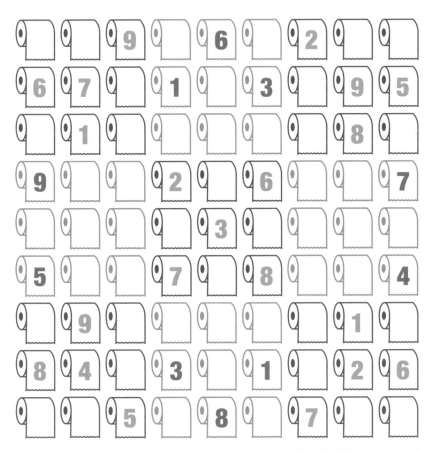

POODOKU
DIFFICULTY LEVEL 💩 💩 💩

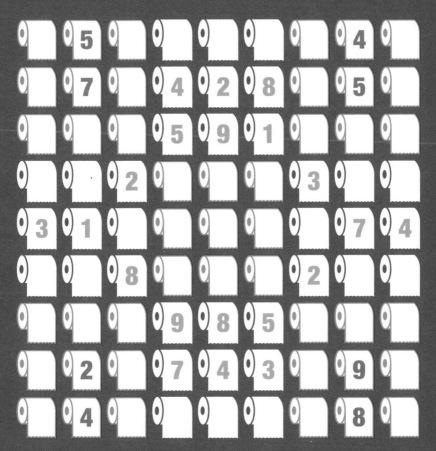

POODOKU
DIFFICULTY LEVEL 💩💩💩

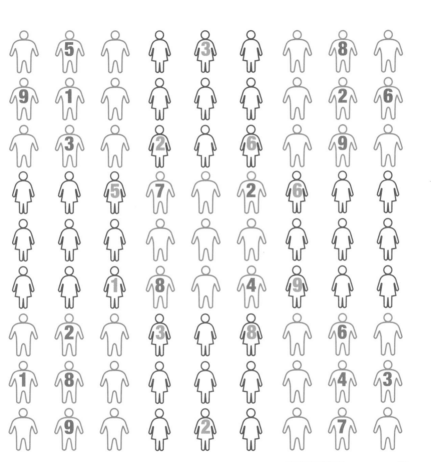

EACH WORD SHOULD APPEAR ONCE IN EVERY ROW, COLUMN AND 3X2 BOX
POO CRAP DUMP SHIT STOOL TURD

POODOKU
DIFFICULTY LEVEL

52 POODOKUS TO DO...

		CRAP	TURD	SHIT	DUMP
		DUMP	STOOL		CRAP
SHIT	CRAP	POO			STOOL
	TURD	STOOL			POO
CRAP		SHIT	POO	STOOL	
		TURD	CRAP	DUMP	SHIT

POODOKU
DIFFICULTY LEVEL 💩💩💩

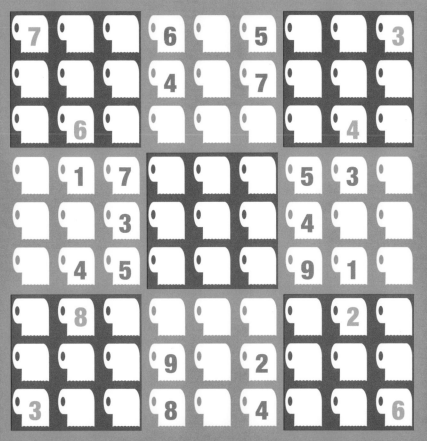

POODOKU
DIFFICULTY LEVEL 💩💩💩

POODOKU
DIFFICULTY LEVEL 💩△△

	PRIVY	DUNNY	KHAZI		JOHN
	JOHN	CAN	BOG	DUNNY	
			CAN	JOHN	KHAZI
	KHAZI		DUNNY	PRIVY	
JOHN	CAN	BOG		KHAZI	
PRIVY	DUNNY	KHAZI		BOG	

POODOKU
DIFFICULTY LEVEL 💩🔺🔺

POODOKU
DIFFICULTY LEVEL ⬤△△

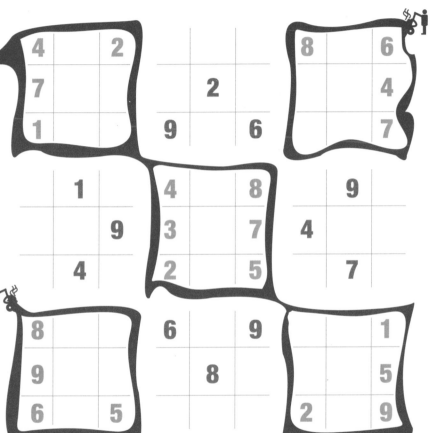

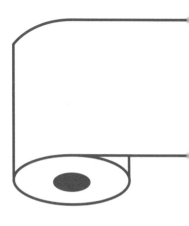

POODOKU
DIFFICULTY LEVEL

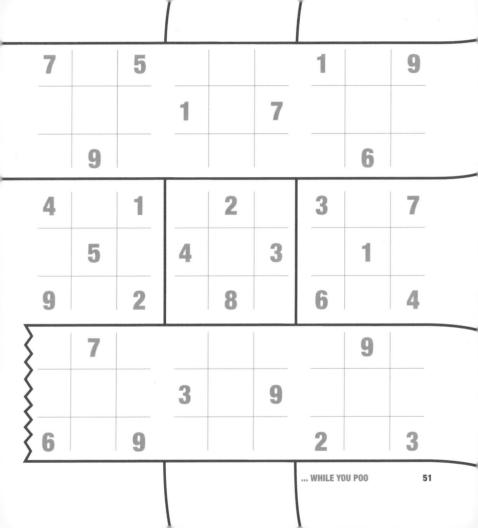

POODOKU
DIFFICULTY LEVEL 💩💩💩

POODOKU
DIFFICULTY LEVEL 💩 💩 🔘

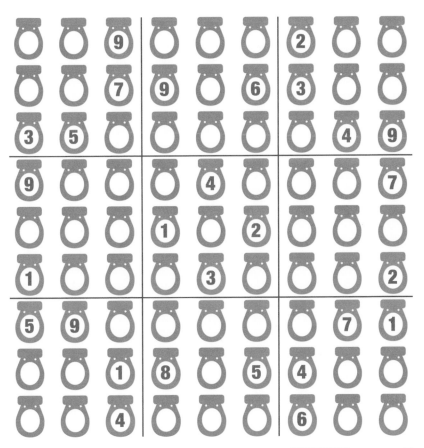

POODOKU
DIFFICULTY LEVEL

POODOKU
DIFFICULTY LEVEL 💩🔳🔳

POODOKU
DIFFICULTY LEVEL 💩💩💩

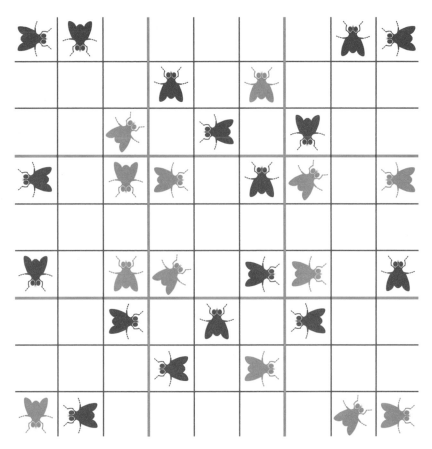

POODOKU
DIFFICULTY LEVEL 💩💩💩

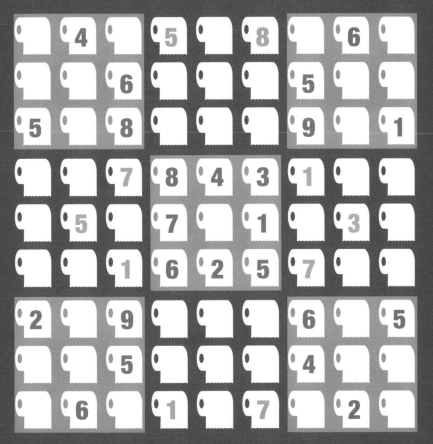

POODOKU
DIFFICULTY LEVEL 💩💩🔾

POODOKU
DIFFICULTY LEVEL 💩💩💩

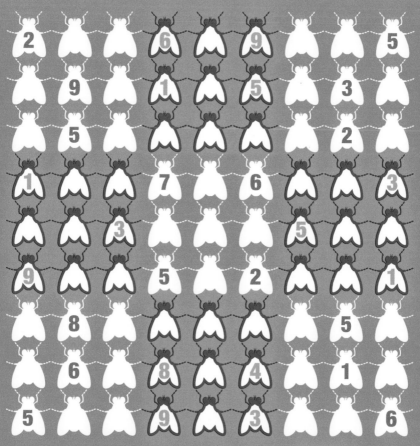

POODOKU
DIFFICULTY LEVEL 💩🔺🔺

POODOKU
DIFFICULTY LEVEL 💩💩💩

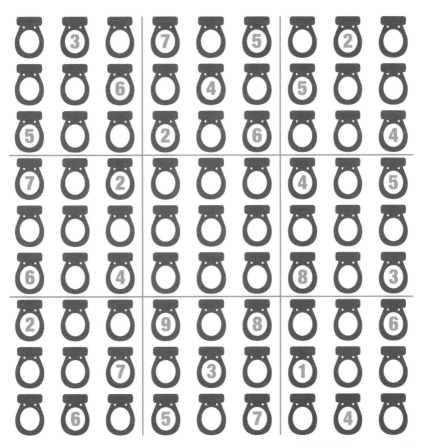

POODOKU
DIFFICULTY LEVEL ♨ ♨ ♨

POODOKU
DIFFICULTY LEVEL

POODOKU
DIFFICULTY LEVEL

	O		E	I	
	L	T	O		
L	O				I
				E	O
	L	T	O		
T				L	T

POODOKU

DIFFICULTY LEVEL 💩🤍🤍

	1	7	6		8	2	9	
5		6				1		8
3		8	7		4	5		9
7		4	9		3	6		2
6		9				7		1
	3	2	5		7	8	6	

POODOKU
DIFFICULTY LEVEL 💩 💩 💩

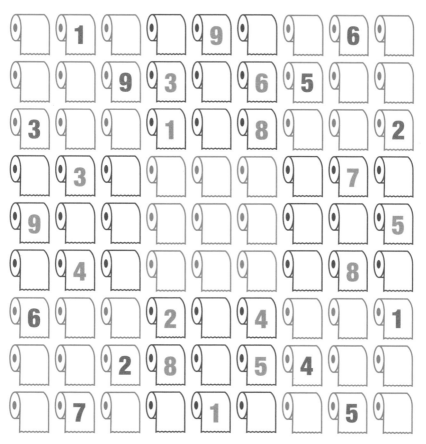

POODOKU
DIFFICULTY LEVEL

			A		E			
	A	K				E		A
A	E						A	K
K			T	E	L			A
K	L						T	K
E			K	E	K			A
A	K						E	E
	K	A				T	K	
			L		A			

POODOKU
DIFFICULTY LEVEL

5		9				4		1
4				6				3
			8	9	4			
	6		2		1		7	
3								2
	2		5		9		3	
			3	1	8			
1				5				8
7		8				3		5

EACH WORD SHOULD APPEAR ONCE IN EVERY ROW, COLUMN AND 3X2 BOX
BUM BUTT REAR TUSH RUMP BEHIND

POODOKU
DIFFICULTY LEVEL

		BUTT	BUM		BEHIND
BUM		BEHIND	RUMP		BUTT
TUSH					REAR
	BUTT	REAR			BUM
	RUMP	BUM			
BUTT	BEHIND	TUSH	REAR		RUMP

POODOKU
DIFFICULTY LEVEL

		3			9			
	1		5		8		2	
2	4			9			8	7
3	8						9	2
		2	9		3	8		
1	7						6	3
4	3			2			7	9
	9		1		4		3	
		6				4		

POODOKU
DIFFICULTY LEVEL

O	O		M	B	
M		T	O	O	T
				M	O
B		O			
O		M	T		B
			O		

POODOKU
DIFFICULTY LEVEL 💩💩💩

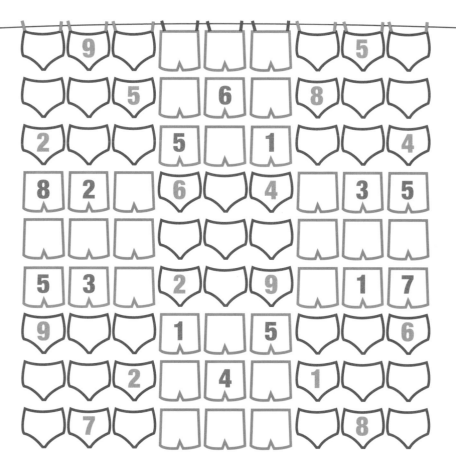

POODOKU
DIFFICULTY LEVEL 💩💩💩

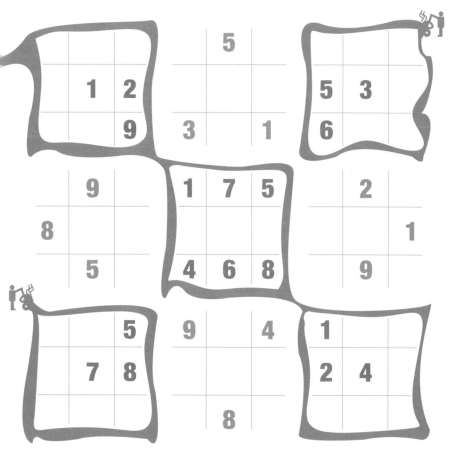

POODOKU
DIFFICULTY LEVEL 💩💩💩

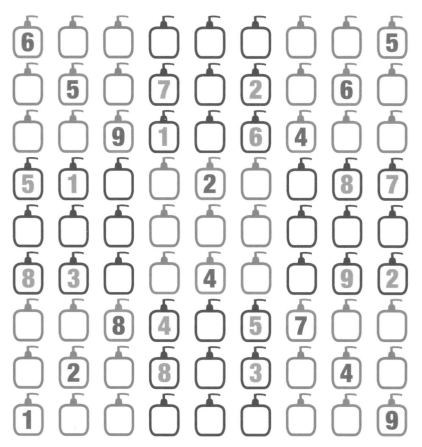

POODOKU
DIFFICULTY LEVEL 💩 △ △

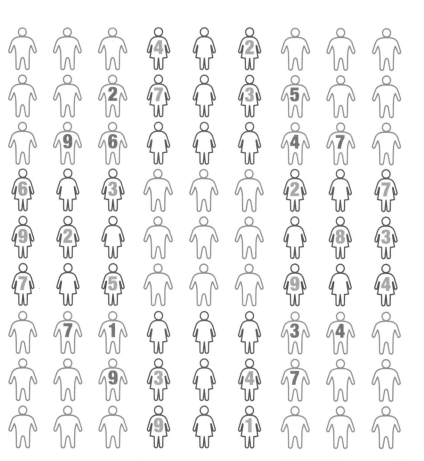

POODOKU
DIFFICULTY LEVEL 💩�

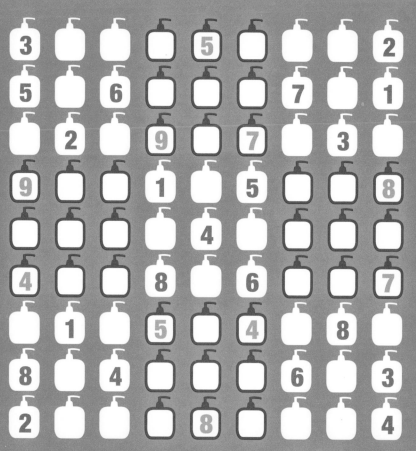

POODOKU
DIFFICULTY LEVEL 💩 🔺 🔺

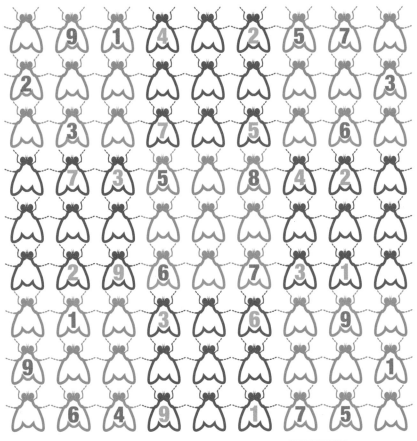

POODOKU
DIFFICULTY LEVEL 💩💩💩

POODOKU
DIFFICULTY LEVEL 💩🤍🤍

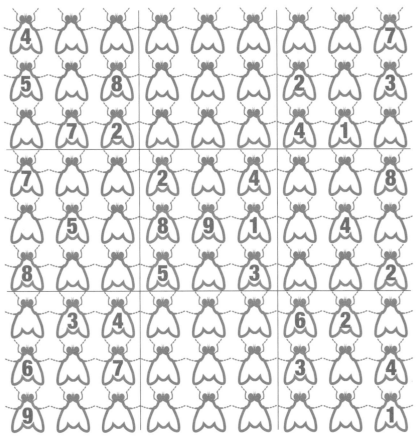

ANSWERS

P4–5

```
6 9 1   5 7 4   2 8 3
2 3 7   8 6 9   5 1 4
5 4 8   2 3 1   7 9 6

8 1 3   7 4 2   9 6 5
9 2 6   1 5 3   4 7 8
4 7 5   6 9 8   1 3 2

7 8 9   4 2 6   3 5 1
1 5 4   3 8 7   6 2 9
3 6 2   9 1 5   8 4 7
```

P6–7

```
3 2 7   1 9 6   4 8 5
8 9 4   3 2 5   7 6 1
1 5 6   7 8 4   9 3 2

4 6 5   8 3 2   1 9 7
2 3 1   6 7 9   5 4 8
9 7 8   4 5 1   6 2 3

7 8 9   5 4 3   2 1 6
6 4 3   2 1 7   8 5 9
5 1 2   9 6 8   3 7 4
```

P8–9

```
4 9 5   2 1 6   3 8 7
6 8 2   3 7 4   5 9 1
1 7 3   5 8 9   2 6 4

2 3 6   8 5 7   1 4 9
9 1 7   4 6 3   8 2 5
8 5 4   1 9 2   7 3 6

7 6 8   9 3 1   4 5 2
3 4 1   6 2 5   9 7 8
5 2 9   7 4 8   6 1 3
```

P10–11

```
5 8 4   6 2 3   1 9 7
7 1 2   9 4 5   6 8 3
9 3 6   7 8 1   4 5 2

4 2 9   1 6 8   7 3 5
3 6 8   5 7 4   9 2 1
1 7 5   3 9 2   8 4 6

6 4 3   8 5 7   2 1 9
8 5 7   2 1 9   3 6 4
2 9 1   4 3 6   5 7 8
```

P12–13

```
7 5 6   4 9 8   1 2 3
1 3 9   2 6 7   5 8 4
8 4 2   5 1 3   7 9 6

4 9 8   3 5 1   2 6 7
2 6 7   8 4 9   3 1 5
3 1 5   7 2 6   8 4 9

6 7 3   1 8 4   9 5 2
5 8 4   9 3 2   6 7 1
9 2 1   6 7 5   4 3 8
```

P14–15

WEE	PEE	WAZ	PISS	TINKLE	URINATE
PISS	TINKLE	URINATE	WEE	WAZ	PEE
WAZ	URINATE	TINKLE	PEE	PISS	WEE
PEE	PISS	WEE	WAZ	URINATE	TINKLE
URINATE	WAZ	PEE	TINKLE	WEE	PISS
TINKLE	WEE	PISS	URINATE	PEE	WAZ

P16–17

```
2 3 9   4 7 5   6 1 8
6 7 4   8 3 1   9 5 2
8 1 5   2 6 9   3 7 4

5 4 1   6 8 2   7 9 3
7 2 3   5 9 4   1 8 6
9 8 6   3 1 7   4 2 5

3 5 7   1 4 8   2 6 9
4 9 8   7 2 6   5 3 1
1 6 2   9 5 3   8 4 7
```

P18–19

P20–21

```
1 7 3   6 4 8   9 5 2
6 5 9   7 3 2   4 1 8
8 4 2   1 5 9   7 6 3

5 3 4   8 2 7   6 9 1
9 2 1   3 6 5   8 7 4
7 6 8   4 9 1   3 2 5

4 1 6   5 7 3   2 8 9
3 9 5   2 8 6   1 4 7
2 8 7   9 1 4   5 3 6
```

P22–23

```
3 1 7   9 5 2   8 4 6
8 5 6   7 3 4   1 9 2
2 9 4   8 1 6   7 3 5

4 2 5   6 7 9   3 8 1
9 8 3   5 2 1   6 7 4
7 6 1   4 8 3   5 2 9

6 7 2   1 4 8   9 5 3
1 3 8   2 9 5   4 6 7
5 4 9   3 6 7   2 1 8
```

P24–25

```
7 5 1   3 6 4   8 2 9
8 2 6   1 9 7   3 4 5
4 3 9   2 8 5   7 6 1

2 9 4   5 1 8   6 3 7
6 7 3   4 2 9   1 5 8
1 8 5   6 7 3   2 9 4

9 1 2   7 4 6   5 8 3
5 6 8   9 3 1   4 7 2
3 4 7   8 5 2   9 1 6
```

P26–27

P28–29

```
762  831  945
459  672  318
813  549  267

527  918  634
638  254  791
941  367  582

384  726  159
176  495  823
295  183  476
```

P30–31

```
A T O   Y L !   A V R
R Y !   T V A   A O L
L V A   O R A   T Y !

T A R   A O L   V ! Y
! A V   R Y T   O L A
Y O L   ! A V   R A T

V ! T   A A Y   L R O
O L A   V ! R   Y T A
A R Y   L T O   ! A V
```

P32–33

```
359  864  271
678  123  495
412  975  683

984  256  137
761  439  852
523  718  964

296  547  318
847  391  526
135  682  749
```

P34–35

```
951  637  842
673  428  159
284  591  637

792  154  368
315  862  974
468  379  215

137  985  426
826  743  591
549  216  783
```

P36–37

```
652  439  781
914  587  326
738  216  594

345  792  618
879  163  452
261  854  937

527  348  169
186  975  243
493  621  875
```

P38–39

STOOL POO CRAP	TURD SHIT DUMP
TURD SHIT DUMP	STOOL POO CRAP
SHIT CRAP POO	DUMP TURD STOOL
DUMP TURD STOOL	SHIT CRAP POO
CRAP DUMP SHIT	POO STOOL TURD
POO STOOL TURD	CRAP DUMP SHIT

P40–41

```
794  615  283
238  497  651
561  328  749

617  249  538
923  581  467
845  763  912

489  176  325
156  932  874
372  854  196
```

P42–43

```
635  971  824
147  283  569
982  654  731

318  569  247
564  732  198
279  148  356

793  826  415
451  397  682
826  415  973
```

P44–45

BOG PRIVY DUNNY	KHAZI CAN JOHN
KHAZI JOHN CAN	BOG DUNNY PRIVY
DUNNY BOG PRIVY	CAN JOHN KHAZI
CAN KHAZI JOHN	DUNNY PRIVY BOG
JOHN CAN BOG	PRIVY KHAZI DUNNY
PRIVY DUNNY KHAZI	JOHN BOG CAN

P46–47

```
687  124  593
951  638  724
342  579  168

718  253  946
569  847  312
234  916  857

475  392  681
893  461  275
126  785  439
```

P48–49

```
492  573  816
763  821  954
158  946  327

217  468  593
589  317  462
346  295  178

824  659  731
931  782  645
675  134  289
```

P50–51

```
745  836  129
286  197  435
193  254  768

461  925  387
857  463  912
932  781  654

378  642  591
524  319  876
619  578  243
```

P52–53
```
954 617 832
321 859 674
687 432 519

132 978 465
569 143 728
748 265 391

496 381 257
273 594 186
815 726 943
```

P54–55
```
819 473 256
427 956 318
356 281 749

962 548 137
735 162 984
148 739 562

593 624 871
671 895 423
284 317 695
```

P56–57
```
251 874 963
376 519 248
948 326 715

192 768 354
684 953 127
735 241 896

427 185 639
519 637 482
863 492 571
```

P58–59
```
851 236 794
974 158 236
236 479 581

623 794 815
418 365 927
795 812 643

142 687 359
369 521 478
587 943 162
```

P60–61

P62–63
```
943 518 267
126 479 583
578 236 941

697 843 152
452 791 836
381 625 794

219 384 675
735 962 418
864 157 329
```

P64–65
```
893 275 416
471 638 925
265 194 387

726 983 541
514 762 893
938 541 762

682 359 174
159 427 638
347 816 259
```

P66–67
```
231 689 475
497 125 638
856 347 129

125 796 843
673 418 592
948 532 761

789 261 354
362 854 917
514 973 286
```

P68–69
```
847 263 591
519 487 236
236 591 874

471 632 985
395 748 612
628 915 347

764 859 123
953 124 768
182 376 459
```

P70–71
```
439 785 621
826 341 579
571 296 384

792 863 415
318 459 267
654 172 893

245 918 736
987 634 152
163 527 948
```

P72–73
```
185 624 397
346 987 215
279 135 486

917 548 623
862 713 549
534 269 178

423 896 751
658 471 932
791 352 864
```

P74–75
```
481 792 365
265 341 789
973 586 214

134 258 697
827 963 541
659 174 823

396 425 178
718 639 452
542 817 936
```

P76–77

T	O	T	E	I	L
E	I	L	T	O	T
L	E	O	T	T	I
T	T	I	L	E	O
I	L	T	O	T	E
O	T	E	I	L	T

P78–79

```
417 638 295
983 251 476
526 479 138

368 724 519
291 865 347
754 913 682

649 382 751
875 146 923
132 597 864
```

P80–81

```
514 792 863
829 346 517
367 158 942

235 981 674
981 467 325
746 523 189

658 234 791
192 875 436
473 619 258
```

P82–83

```
T A K A L E K A E
L A K E K A E A T
A E E A T K L A K
K A A T E L K E A
K L E A A A E T K
E T A K E K A L A
A K L K A T A E E
A K A E A E T K L
E E T L K A A K A
```

P84–85

```
589 723 461
472 165 983
631 894 257

965 231 874
317 486 592
824 579 136

256 318 749
143 957 628
798 642 315
```

P86–87

RUMP TUSH BUTT	BUM REAR BEHIND
BUM REAR BEHIND	RUMP TUSH BUTT
TUSH BUM RUMP	BUTT BEHIND REAR
BEHIND BUTT REAR	TUSH RUMP BUM
REAR RUMP BUM	BEHIND BUTT TUSH
BUTT BEHIND TUSH	REAR BUM RUMP

P88–89

```
863 217 954
917 548 326
245 396 187

384 651 792
652 973 841
179 482 563

431 825 679
798 164 235
526 739 418
```

P90–91

O	O	T	M	B	T
M	B	T	O	O	T
T	T	O	B	M	O
B	M	O	T	T	O
O	T	M	T	O	B
T	O	B	O	T	M

P92–93

```
394 872 651
715 463 829
268 591 374

827 614 935
149 357 268
536 289 417

983 125 746
652 748 193
471 936 582
```

P94–95

```
346 752 918
712 896 534
589 341 672

493 175 826
867 239 451
251 468 793

635 924 187
978 613 245
124 587 369
```

P96–97

```
673 984 215
451 732 968
289 156 473

514 629 387
962 378 154
837 541 692

398 415 726
726 893 541
145 267 839
```

P98–99

```
157 492 836
842 763 591
396 815 472

683 149 257
924 657 183
715 238 964

271 586 349
569 324 718
438 971 625
```

P100–101

379	451	862
546	328	791
128	967	435

962	175	348
785	243	916
431	896	527

617	534	289
894	712	653
253	689	174

P102–103

691	432	578
257	869	143
438	715	269

173	598	426
546	123	987
829	647	315

712	356	894
985	274	631
364	981	752

P104–105

498	137	256
261	594	387
357	682	149

124	376	598
579	248	631
683	915	472

942	751	863
715	863	924
836	429	715

P106–107

461	325	987
598	147	263
372	689	415

719	264	538
253	891	746
846	573	192

134	758	629
687	912	354
925	436	871

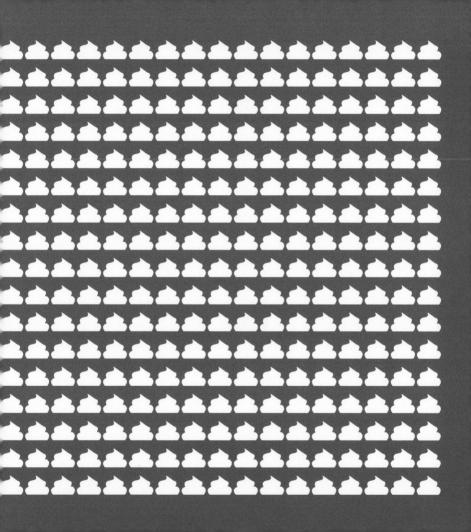

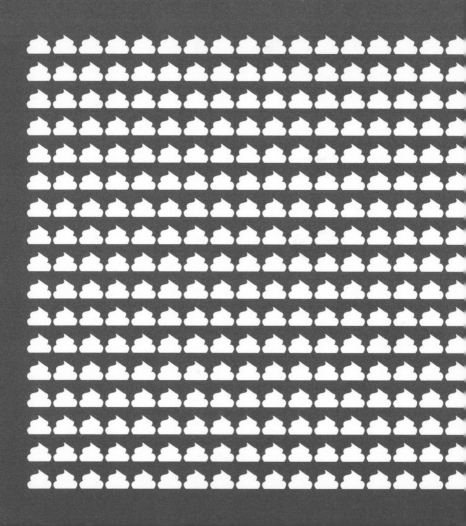